MAD LIBS®

OFF-THE-WALL MAD LIBS

By Roger Pric

PRICE STERN SLOAN

Copyright © 2001, 1988, 1982, 1970 by Price Stern Sloan.
All rights reserved.
Published by Price Stern Sloan, a division of
Penguin Putnam Books for Young Readers, 345 Hudson St., NY 10014.

ISBN 0-8431-0108-3

2007 PRINTING

MAD LIBS
INSTRUCTIONS

MAD LIBS® is a game for people who don't like games!
It can be played by one, two, three, four, or forty.

• RIDICULOUSLY SIMPLE DIRECTIONS

In this tablet you will find stories containing blank spaces where words are
left out. One player, the READER, selects one of these stories. The READER
does not tell anyone what the story is about. Instead, he/she asks the other
players, the WRITERS, to give him/her words. These words are used to fill
in the blank spaces in the story.

• TO PLAY

The READER asks each WRITER in turn to call out a word—an adjective or
a noun or whatever the space calls for—and uses them to fill in the blank
spaces in the story. The result is a MAD LIBS® game.

When the READER then reads the completed MAD LIBS® game to the other
players, they will discover that they have written a story that is fantastic,
screamingly funny, shocking, silly, crazy, or just plain dumb—depending
upon which words each WRITER called out.

• EXAMPLE (*Before* and *After*)

"_____!" he said _____
      EXCLAMATION   ADVERB

as he jumped into his convertible _____ and
                                 NOUN

drove off with his _____ wife.
                    ADJECTIVE

"*Ouch!*_____!" he said *Stupidly*_____
      EXCLAMATION   ADVERB

as he jumped into his convertible *cat*_____ and
                                 NOUN

drove off with his *brave*_____ wife.
                    ADJECTIVE

In case you have forgotten what adjectives, adverbs, nouns, and verbs are, here is a quick review:

An ADJECTIVE describes something or somebody. *Lumpy, soft, ugly, messy,* and *short* are adjectives.

An ADVERB tells how something is done. It modifies a verb and usually ends in "ly." *Modestly, stupidly, greedily,* and *carefully* are adverbs.

A NOUN is the name of a person, place or thing. *Sidewalk, umbrella, bridle, bathtub,* and *nose* are nouns.

A VERB is an action word. *Run, pitch, jump,* and *swim* are verbs. Put the verbs in past tense if the directions say PAST TENSE. *Ran, pitched, jumped,* and *swam* are verbs in the past tense.

When we ask for a PLACE, we mean any sort of place: a country or city *(Spain, Cleveland)* or a room *(bathroom, kitchen.)*

An EXCLAMATION or SILLY WORD is any sort of funny sound, gasp, grunt, or outcry, like *Wow!, Ouch!, Whomp!, Ick!,* and *Gadzooks!*

When we ask for specific words, like a NUMBER, a COLOR, an ANIMAL, or a PART OF THE BODY, we mean a word that is one of those things, like *seven, blue, horse,* or *head.*

When we ask for a PLURAL, it means more than one. For example, *cat* pluralized is *cats.*

MAD LIBS® is fun to play with friends, but you can also play it by yourself! To begin with, DO NOT look at the story on the page below. Fill in the blanks on this page with the words called for. Then, using the words you have selected, fill in the blank spaces in the story.

Now you've created your own hilarious MAD LIBS® game!

PAUL REVERE

STATE_____

ADJECTIVE_____

NOUN _____

NATIONALITY _____

NOUN _____

TYPE OF LIQUID _____

PLACE _____

NOUN _____

NOUN _____

NOUN _____

ADVERB_____

PLURAL NOUN _____

SAME PLURAL NOUN _____

CELEBRITY (MALE)_____

From OFF-THE-WALL MAD LIBS® • Copyright © 2001, 1988, 1982, 1970 by Price Stern Sloan, a division of Penguin Putnam Books for Young Readers, New York.

MAD LIBS
PAUL REVERE

Paul Revere was born in Boston, _____ , in 1735.
STATE

His father taught him to work with metals, and he soon became a/an

_____   _____ . He was a soldier in the
ADJECTIVE   NOUN

French and _____ War and was at the famous Boston
NATIONALITY

_____ Party when Americans dressed as Indians dumped tons of
NOUN

_____ into the ocean. On April 18, 1775, Paul Revere
TYPE OF LIQUID

waited in _____ for a signal light from a church tower. The
PLACE

signal was to be one if by _____ , two if by _____ .
NOUN   NOUN

When he got the message, he mounted his faithful _____
NOUN

and rode off _____ . On the way, he kept yelling, "The
ADVERB

_____ are coming! The _____ are coming!"
PLURAL NOUN   SAME PLURAL NOUN

This was the beginning of the American War for Independence from

King _____ .
CELEBRITY (MALE)

MAD LIBS® is fun to play with friends, but you can also play it by yourself! To begin with, DO NOT look at the story on the page below. Fill in the blanks on this page with the words called for. Then, using the words you have selected, fill in the blank spaces in the story.

Now you've created your own hilarious MAD LIBS® game!

ELIZABETH THE FIRST

NOUN _____

ADJECTIVE (SUPERLATIVE)_____

NOUN _____

ADJECTIVE_____

ADJECTIVE_____

ADVERB_____

NATIONALITY _____

CELEBRITY _____

ANOTHER CELEBRITY _____

NAME OF PERSON _____

ADJECTIVE_____

MAD LIBS®
ELIZABETH THE FIRST

Elizabeth, the Tudor _____ of England, was probably the
                            NOUN

_____ ruler the British ever had. Elizabeth was the
ADJECTIVE (SUPERLATIVE)

daughter of Henry the Eighth and Anne Boleyn. Later, Anne had

her _____ chopped off by Henry.
            NOUN

Elizabeth was born in 1533 and became queen when she was 25. She

was a/an _____ Protestant and persecuted the _____
              ADJECTIVE   ADJECTIVE

Catholics _____. In 1588, the _____ Armada
                ADVERB   NATIONALITY

attacked England. But the English fleet, commanded by _____
                                                              CELEBRITY

and _____, defeated them. Elizabeth ruled for 45 years,
    ANOTHER CELEBRITY

and during her reign England prospered and produced Shakespeare,

Francis Bacon, and _____. Elizabeth never married,
                        NAME OF PERSON

which is why she is sometimes called the _____ Queen.
                                                ADJECTIVE

MAD LIBS® is fun to play with friends, but you can also play it by yourself! To begin with, DO NOT look at the story on the page below. Fill in the blanks on this page with the words called for. Then, using the words you have selected, fill in the blank spaces in the story.

Now you've created your own hilarious MAD LIBS® game!

REPORT BY STUDENT PROTEST COMMITTEE

SCHOOL _____

ADJECTIVE_____

PLURAL NOUN _____

PERSON IN ROOM (MALE)_____

PART OF THE BODY _____

ARTICLE OF CLOTHING_____

PLURAL NOUN _____

NOUN _____

NOUN _____

ADJECTIVE_____

ADJECTIVE_____

PLURAL NOUN _____

MAD LIBS®
REPORT BY STUDENT
PROTEST COMMITTEE

Fellow Students of ＿＿＿＿＿＿! We the members of the Students
　　　　　　　　　　　SCHOOL

for a/an ＿＿＿＿＿＿＿ Society are meeting here to decide what
　　　　　ADJECTIVE

action to take about the Dean of ＿＿＿＿＿＿＿. He has just fired
　　　　　　　　　　　　　　　　　PLURAL NOUN

our friend, Professor ＿＿＿＿＿＿＿＿＿＿＿, because he wore his
　　　　　　　　　　　PERSON IN ROOM (MALE)

＿＿＿＿＿＿＿＿＿＿ long, and because he dressed in a/an
PART OF THE BODY

＿＿＿＿＿＿＿＿＿ and wore old ＿＿＿＿＿＿＿. Next week,
ARTICLE OF CLOTHING　　　　　　PLURAL NOUN

we are going to protest by taking over the ＿＿＿＿＿＿＿＿＿
　　　　　　　　　　　　　　　　　　　　　　NOUN

building and kidnapping the Assistant ＿＿＿＿＿＿＿. We also
　　　　　　　　　　　　　　　　　　　NOUN

will demand that all students have the right to wear ＿＿＿＿＿＿
　　　　　　　　　　　　　　　　　　　　　　　ADJECTIVE

hair and ＿＿＿＿＿＿＿＿＿ beards. Remember our slogan:
　　　　　ADJECTIVE

"Down with ＿＿＿＿＿＿＿."
　　　　　　PLURAL NOUN

MAD LIBS® is fun to play with friends, but you can also play it by yourself! To begin with, DO NOT look at the story on the page below. Fill in the blanks on this page with the words called for. Then, using the words you have selected, fill in the blank spaces in the story.

Now you've created your own hilarious MAD LIBS® game!

ALEXANDER THE GREAT

NOUN _____

NOUN _____

CELEBRITY _____

NOUN _____

CELEBRITY _____

A PLACE _____

NOUN _____

SILLY WORD_____

PLURAL NOUN _____

TYPE OF LIQUID _____

PART OF THE BODY _____

PLURAL NOUN _____

MAD LIBS®
ALEXANDER THE GREAT

In 356 B.C., Phillip of Macedonia, the ruler of a province in northern

Greece, became the father of a bouncing baby _____
                                                    NOUN

named Alexander. Alexander's teacher was Aristotle, the famous

_____ . When he was 20 years old, his father was murdered
   NOUN

by _____ , after which he became _____ of all
      CELEBRITY   NOUN

Macedonia. In 334, he invaded Persia and defeated _____
                                                        CELEBRITY

at the battle of _____ . Later, at Arbela, he won his most
                    A PLACE

important victory, over Darius the Third. This made him _____
                                                              NOUN

_____ over all Persians. Then he marched to India, and
   SILLY WORD

many of his _____ died. After that, Alexander began
               PLURAL NOUN

drinking too much _____ , and at the age of 33, he died
                      TYPE OF LIQUID

of an infection in the _____ . His last words are reported
                         PART OF THE BODY

to have been, "There are no more _____ to conquer."
                                       PLURAL NOUN

From OFF-THE-WALL MAD LIBS® • Copyright © 2001, 1988, 1982, 1970 by Price Stern Sloan,
a division of Penguin Putnam Books for Young Readers, New York.

MAD LIBS® is fun to play with friends, but you can also play it by yourself! To begin with, DO NOT look at the story on the page below. Fill in the blanks on this page with the words called for. Then, using the words you have selected, fill in the blank spaces in the story.

Now you've created your own hilarious MAD LIBS® game!

EASTER

PLURAL NOUN _____

NUMBER _____

ADJECTIVE _____

NOUN _____

TYPE OF GAME _____

ADJECTIVE _____

PLURAL NOUN _____

ADJECTIVE _____

ADJECTIVE _____

TYPE OF LIQUID _____

NOUN _____

ANOTHER TYPE OF LIQUID _____

ADJECTIVE _____

MAD LIBS®
EASTER

Spring vacation usually falls around Easter time. The schools are

closed and all the _____ get _____ weeks off.
                        PLURAL NOUN   NUMBER

The _____ teachers also get a vacation. There are a lot of
        ADJECTIVE

things to do during Easter vacation. Some kids loaf around and

watch the _____. Others get outside and play _____,
             NOUN   TYPE OF GAME

while more ambitious students spend their time studying

their _____ books so they will grow up to become
          ADJECTIVE

_____. Little kids also color _____ eggs.
  PLURAL NOUN   ADJECTIVE

Here's how you color an egg: First, mix a package of _____
                                                          ADJECTIVE

dye in a bowl full of _____. Then, dip a/an _____
                       TYPE OF LIQUID   NOUN

in the bowl and rinse it off with _____. Then, after
                                  ANOTHER TYPE OF LIQUID

it dries, you can paint on it with a brush. Then you show it to your

friends, who will say, "Boy, what a/an _____ egg!"
                                           ADJECTIVE

MAD LIBS® is fun to play with friends, but you can also play it by yourself! To begin with, DO NOT look at the story on the page below. Fill in the blanks on this page with the words called for. Then, using the words you have selected, fill in the blank spaces in the story.

Now you've created your own hilarious MAD LIBS® game!

ALBERT EINSTEIN

CELEBRITY (MALE) _____

CELEBRITY (FEMALE) _____

NOUN _____

PLURAL NOUN _____

ADJECTIVE _____

PLURAL NOUN _____

ADJECTIVE _____

PLURAL NOUN _____

NOUN _____

A PLACE _____

PLURAL NOUN _____

NOUN _____

PROFESSION (PLURAL) _____

MAD LIBS
ALBERT EINSTEIN

Albert Einstein, the son of _____ and _____,
CELEBRITY (MALE)   CELEBRITY (FEMALE)

was born in Ulm, Germany, in 1879. In 1902, he had a job as

assistant _____ in the Swiss patent office and attended
NOUN

the University of Zurich. There he began studying atoms, molecules,

and _____. He developed his famous theory of
PLURAL NOUN

_____ relativity, which expanded the phenomena of sub-
ADJECTIVE

atomic _____ and _____ magnetism. In 1921,
PLURAL NOUN   ADJECTIVE

he won the Nobel prize for _____ and was director of
PLURAL NOUN

theoretical physics at the Kaiser Wilhelm _____ in Berlin.
NOUN

In 1933, when Hitler became Chancellor of _____,
A PLACE

Einstein came to America to take a post at Princeton Institute for

_____, where his theories helped America devise the first
PLURAL NOUN

atomic _____. There is no question about it: Einstein was
NOUN

one of the most brilliant _____ of our time.
PROFESSION (PLURAL)

MAD LIBS® is fun to play with friends, but you can also play it by yourself! To begin with, DO NOT look at the story on the page below. Fill in the blanks on this page with the words called for. Then, using the words you have selected, fill in the blank spaces in the story.

Now you've created your own hilarious MAD LIBS® game!

ROCK MUSIC

LAST NAME OF PERSON _____

ANOTHER LAST NAME_____

ADJECTIVE_____

PLURAL NOUN _____

PLURAL NOUN _____

ANIMAL (PLURAL) _____

CELEBRITY _____

PLURAL NOUN _____

PLURAL NOUN _____

NOUN _____

NOUN _____

PLURAL NOUN _____

MAD LIBS®
ROCK MUSIC

Young people today would rather listen to a good rock music concert

than to Johann Sebastian _____ or to Ludvig von
                          LAST NAME OF PERSON

_____. Rock music is played by _____ groups
ANOTHER LAST NAME   ADJECTIVE

of young men who wear their hair below their _____. They
                                              PLURAL NOUN

also wear very odd and colorful _____ and often have beards.
                                 PLURAL NOUN

The groups have attractive names such as "The _____"
                                               ANIMAL (PLURAL)

or "_____ and The Three _____." They usually
     CELEBRITY   PLURAL NOUN

play electric _____. One member of the group usually sits
               PLURAL NOUN

on a raised platform and sets the rhythm by beating his _____.
                                                          NOUN

The songs they sing are mostly about some fellow who has been

rejected by his _____. They are very sad, and when young
                 NOUN

girls hear them, they often get tears in their _____.
                                                PLURAL NOUN

MAD LIBS® is fun to play with friends, but you can also play it by yourself! To begin with, DO NOT look at the story on the page below. Fill in the blanks on this page with the words called for. Then, using the words you have selected, fill in the blank spaces in the story.

Now you've created your own hilarious MAD LIBS® game!

BENJAMIN FRANKLIN

VERB _____

PLURAL NOUN _____

NOUN _____

NOUN _____

ADJECTIVE _____

ADVERB _____

ADJECTIVE _____

NOUN _____

NOUN _____

PLURAL NOUN _____

ADJECTIVE _____

SILLY WORD _____

MAD LIBS®
BENJAMIN FRANKLIN

Benjamin Franklin left school at the age of 10 to _____ for

VERB

his father, who made candles, soap, and _____ in a little shop

PLURAL NOUN

in Boston. In 1723, when Franklin was 17, he went to Philadelphia

carrying a loaf of _____ under his arm. He got a job as

NOUN

an apprentice _____ and soon became the editor of the

NOUN

Pennsylvania Gazette, a/an _____ publication. He worked

ADJECTIVE

_____ and in 1732, he published the _____ book

ADVERB   ADJECTIVE

called "Poor Richard's _____." He then became interested

NOUN

in science and, during a thunderstorm, he flew a/an _____

NOUN

attached to a string and proved that lightning and electricity were the

same thing. He also invented the harmonica, bifocal _____,

PLURAL NOUN

and started our postal service. In 1776, he became the American

Ambassador to France and did much to help the _____ cause

ADJECTIVE

of American liberty. Franklin was one of the most famous signers of

the Declaration of _____.

SILLY WORD

From OFF-THE-WALL MAD LIBS® • Copyright © 2001, 1988, 1982, 1970 by Price Stern Sloan,
a division of Penguin Putnam Books for Young Readers, New York.

MAD LIBS® is fun to play with friends, but you can also play it by yourself! To begin with, DO NOT look at the story on the page below. Fill in the blanks on this page with the words called for. Then, using the words you have selected, fill in the blank spaces in the story.

Now you've created your own hilarious MAD LIBS® game!

NAPOLEON

NOUN _____

NOUN _____

ADJECTIVE_____

ADJECTIVE_____

ADJECTIVE_____

NOUN _____

ITALIAN WORD _____

PLURAL NOUN _____

ADJECTIVE_____

PLURAL NOUN _____

PLURAL NOUN _____

PLURAL NOUN _____

VERB (PAST TENSE)_____

OCCUPATION _____

ADJECTIVE_____

CITY _____

MAD LIBS®
NAPOLEON

Although he was Emperor of France, Napoleon Bonaparte was actually a Corsican, born on a small _____ in the Mediterranean
NOUN

Sea. When he was just 10 years old, Napoleon was sent to a military

_____ school in France, where his _____ stature
NOUN   ADJECTIVE

earned him the nickname of "The _____ Corporal." At 24,
ADJECTIVE

he was made a/an _____ General and married Josephine,
ADJECTIVE

the daughter of a well-known Parisian _____. Soon after
NOUN

that, he defeated the Italians at _____ and in 1804 was
ITALIAN WORD

proclaimed Emperor of all the _____. But he made a/an
PLURAL NOUN

_____ mistake and attacked Russia. He reached Moscow, but
ADJECTIVE

the _____ had burned all their _____ and his men
PLURAL NOUN   PLURAL NOUN

got frozen _____. In 1914, he was _____ and
PLURAL NOUN   VERB (PAST TENSE)

sent to Elba. But a year later, he came back to France and for 100 days

was again the _____. However, he was defeated at Waterloo
OCCUPATION

and imprisoned on the island of St. Helena, a/an _____ place
ADJECTIVE

which resembled _____.
CITY

From OFF-THE-WALL MAD LIBS® • Copyright © 2001, 1988, 1982, 1970 by Price Stern Sloan,
a division of Penguin Putnam Books for Young Readers, New York.

MAD LIBS® is fun to play with friends, but you can also play it by yourself! To begin with, DO NOT look at the story on the page below. Fill in the blanks on this page with the words called for. Then, using the words you have selected, fill in the blank spaces in the story.

Now you've created your own hilarious MAD LIBS® game!

OUR SCHOOL

SCHOOL _____

ADJECTIVE (SUPERLATIVE)_____

ADJECTIVE_____

NUMBER _____

NUMBER _____

PLURAL NOUN _____

SAME PLURAL NOUN _____

ADJECTIVE_____

PLURAL NOUN _____

NOUN _____

TYPE OF LIQUID _____

CELEBRITY _____

NOUN _____

NOUN _____

ADJECTIVE_____

MAD LIBS®
OUR SCHOOL

_____ is one of America's _____
SCHOOL   ADJECTIVE (SUPERLATIVE)

institutions of _____ learning. The student body is composed
                  ADJECTIVE

of _____ males and _____ _____ . The
    NUMBER   NUMBER   PLURAL NOUN

_____ get the best grades. Students can eat lunch in
SAME PLURAL NOUN

the _____ school cafeteria, which features boiled _____
     ADJECTIVE   PLURAL NOUN

and _____ sandwiches, with all the _____ they can
     NOUN   TYPE OF LIQUID

drink, for only 74 cents. The principal of the school, _____ ,
                                                        CELEBRITY

is raising money to build a new _____ laboratory and a new
                                 NOUN

football _____ . Any student who goes to this school can
         NOUN

consider himself very _____ .
                       ADJECTIVE

MAD LIBS® is fun to play with friends, but you can also play it by yourself! To begin with, DO NOT look at the story on the page below. Fill in the blanks on this page with the words called for. Then, using the words you have selected, fill in the blank spaces in the story.

Now you've created your own hilarious MAD LIBS® game!

CHARLEMAGNE

ADJECTIVE_____

NATIONALITY (PLURAL) _____

NOUN _____

ADJECTIVE_____

NOUN _____

NOUN _____

PLURAL NOUN _____

PLURAL NOUN _____

TOWN_____

ADJECTIVE_____

PLURAL NOUN _____

ADJECTIVE_____

MAD LIBS®
CHARLEMAGNE

Charlemagne was the _____ King of the Franks and
                          ADJECTIVE

_____ . In 800 A.D., he was crowned Emperor of the
NATIONALITY (PLURAL)

Holy Roman _____ by Pope Leo the Third. He was born in
                NOUN

742. His father was Pepin the _____ , and his grandfather
                                  ADJECTIVE

was Charles the _____ . Charlemagne converted thousands
                    NOUN

of Saxons, who were _____ worshippers, to Christianity. He
                          NOUN

converted them by cutting off their _____ and setting fire
                                        PLURAL NOUN

to their _____ . In 778, he invaded Spain, but was defeated
            PLURAL NOUN

by the Moors at _____ . Charlemagne was uneducated, but
                    TOWN

he had great respect for education and established many _____
                                                            ADJECTIVE

schools. And he was known for the justice of his _____ and
                                                    PLURAL NOUN

his kindness to _____ people.
                    ADJECTIVE

MAD LIBS® is fun to play with friends, but you can also play it by yourself! To begin with, DO NOT look at the story on the page below. Fill in the blanks on this page with the words called for. Then, using the words you have selected, fill in the blank spaces in the story.

Now you've created your own hilarious MAD LIBS® game!

GEORGE WASHINGTON CARVER

ADJECTIVE _____

NOUN _____

PLURAL NOUN _____

NOUN _____

PLURAL NOUN _____

TYPE OF FOOD _____

PLACE _____

ADJECTIVE _____

PLURAL NOUN _____

MAD LIBS®
GEORGE WASHINGTON CARVER

George Washington Carver was a very _____ African American
                                     ADJECTIVE

scientist. He was born a/an _____ in Missouri and graduated
                            NOUN

from Iowa State College with high _____. He then worked at
                                  PLURAL NOUN

Tuskegee Institute as head of the _____ department and did
                                  NOUN

much research in the field of _____. He discovered many
                              PLURAL NOUN

new uses for the peanut, the soybean, and the _____.
                                              TYPE OF FOOD

He also improved the production of cotton and helped the entire

economy of _____. George Washington Carver was looked
           PLACE

up to as an inspiration by all _____ people. His death in 1943
                               ADJECTIVE

was a loss to science and to _____ everywhere.
                             PLURAL NOUN

MAD LIBS® is fun to play with friends, but you can also play it by yourself! To begin with, DO NOT look at the story on the page below. Fill in the blanks on this page with the words called for. Then, using the words you have selected, fill in the blank spaces in the story.

Now you've created your own hilarious MAD LIBS® game!

HOW TO BE
A PHOTOGRAPHER

ADJECTIVE _____

PLURAL NOUN _____

PLURAL NOUN _____

ADJECTIVE _____

NOUN _____

NOUN _____

ADJECTIVE _____

NOUN _____

PLURAL NOUN _____

PLURAL NOUN _____

ADVERB _____

NUMBER _____

MAD LIBS®
HOW TO BE
A PHOTOGRAPHER

Many ___fat___ photographers make big money photographing
        ADJECTIVE

___bootys___ and beautiful ___noodles___. They sell the prints
PLURAL NOUN   *PLURAL NOUN*

to ___playboy___ magazines or to agencies who use them in
      ADJECTIVE

___butter___ advertisements. To be a photographer, you have to
    NOUN

have a/an ___pet rock___ camera. You also need a/an ___fat___
            NOUN   *ADJECTIVE*

meter and filters and a special close-up ___stool___. Then you
                                            NOUN

either hire professional ___barber___ or go out and snap candid
                            PLURAL NOUN

pictures of ordinary ___books___. But if you want to have a
                        PLURAL NOUN

career, you must study very ___food___ for at least ___500___ years.
                              ADVERB   *NUMBER*

MAD LIBS® is fun to play with friends, but you can also play it by yourself! To begin with, DO NOT look at the story on the page below. Fill in the blanks on this page with the words called for. Then, using the words you have selected, fill in the blank spaces in the story.

Now you've created your own hilarious MAD LIBS® game!

JULIUS CAESAR

LETTER OF THE ALPHABET _____

ADJECTIVE_____

PLURAL NOUN _____

ADVERB_____

GEOGRAPHICAL LOCATION _____

OCCUPATION _____

PART OF THE BODY_____

NOUN _____

ITALIAN WORD _____

NOUN _____

NOUN _____

FAMOUS PERSON (ITALIAN)_____

MAD LIBS®
JULIUS CAESAR

Julius Caesar was born in 102 B. _____ . He was a/an
<u>LETTER OF THE ALPHABET</u>

_____ general, and between 49 and 58 B.C. he defeated
<u>ADJECTIVE</u>

the Gauls, the Goths, and the _____ . After that, he
<u>PLURAL NOUN</u>

_____ became more famous and defeated Pompey at the battle
<u>ADVERB</u>

of _____ at Pharsala. The Romans then elected him
<u>GEOGRAPHICAL LOCATION</u>

permanent _____ , and he used to walk around wearing
<u>OCCUPATION</u>

a circlet of ivy leaves on his _____ . Then Caesar went to
<u>PART OF THE BODY</u>

Egypt, where he met Cleopatra, the teenage Egyptian _____ .
<u>NOUN</u>

When he conquered the Syrians in 46 B.C., he sent back a message

saying, "Veni, vedi, _____ ." In 44 B.C., a soothsayer told Caesar
<u>ITALIAN WORD</u>

to "Beware the Ides of _____ ," but he ignored the warning
<u>NOUN</u>

and in March he was stabbed in the _____ by a group of
<u>NOUN</u>

senators. His last words were, "Et tu _____ ?"
<u>FAMOUS PERSON (ITALIAN)</u>

MAD LIBS® is fun to play with friends, but you can also play it by yourself! To begin with, DO NOT look at the story on the page below. Fill in the blanks on this page with the words called for. Then, using the words you have selected, fill in the blank spaces in the story.

Now you've created your own hilarious MAD LIBS® game!

LITTLE RED RIDING HOOD

COLOR_____

PLURAL NOUN _____

ADJECTIVE_____

EXCLAMATION_____

SILLY WORD_____

VERB (PAST TENSE)_____

PLURAL NOUN _____

VERB _____

PLURAL NOUN _____

VERB _____

PLURAL NOUN _____

MAD LIBS
LITTLE RED RIDING HOOD

One day, Little _____ Riding Hood was going through the
                        COLOR

forest carrying a basket of _____ for her grandmother.
                                PLURAL NOUN

Suddenly, she met a big _____ wolf. "_____!"
                            ADJECTIVE   EXCLAMATION

said the wolf. "Where are you going, little _____?"
                                                SILLY WORD

"I'm going to my grandmother's house," she said. Then the wolf

_____ away. When Miss Riding Hood got to her grand-
   VERB (PAST TENSE)

mother's house, the wolf was in bed dressed like her grandmother.

"My, Grandmother," she said, "What big _____ you have."
                                            PLURAL NOUN

"The better to _____ you with," said the wolf. "And Grand-
                    VERB

mother," she said, "What big _____ you have." The wolf said,
                                PLURAL NOUN

"The better to _____ you with." And then she said, "What
                    VERB

big _____ you have, Grandmother." But the wolf said
        PLURAL NOUN

nothing. He had just died of indigestion from eating Grandmother.

MAD LIBS® is fun to play with friends, but you can also play it by yourself! To begin with, DO NOT look at the story on the page below. Fill in the blanks on this page with the words called for. Then, using the words you have selected, fill in the blank spaces in the story.

Now you've created your own hilarious MAD LIBS® game!

INTRODUCTION TO A KIDDY SHOW

ADJECTIVE_____

PERSON IN ROOM _____

NUMBER _____

PLURAL NOUN _____

ANIMAL _____

TYPE OF BIRD _____

NONSENSE WORD _____

NOUN _____

LANGUAGE _____

NOUN _____

NUMBER _____

ADJECTIVE_____

MAD LIBS®
INTRODUCTION TO
A KIDDY SHOW

Hi there, all you _____ little boys and girls! This is your
ADJECTIVE

old TV buddy, _____ , with another _____-hour
PERSON IN ROOM   NUMBER

program of fun and films and _____ for all of you. And we
PLURAL NOUN

have a lot of great cartoons and videos. We will start with a cartoon

about Mickey _____ and Donald _____. Then
ANIMAL   TYPE OF BIRD

we'll have a commercial for a new toy called _____.
NONSENSE WORD

It will teach you how to build a _____ and how to speak
NOUN

_____ before you even start school. Next, we'll have a
LANGUAGE

cartoon about Bullwinkle and Rocky, the Flying _____. And
NOUN

after that, _____ more _____ commercials. Wow!
NUMBER   ADJECTIVE

MAD LIBS® is fun to play with friends, but you can also play it by yourself! To begin with, DO NOT look at the story on the page below. Fill in the blanks on this page with the words called for. Then, using the words you have selected, fill in the blank spaces in the story.

Now you've created your own hilarious MAD LIBS® game!

THE THREE LITTLE PIGS

ADJECTIVE_____

PLURAL NOUN _____

ADVERB_____

PLURAL NOUN _____

ADJECTIVE_____

PLURAL NOUN _____

TYPE OF LIQUID _____

VERB (PAST TENSE)_____

VERB (PAST TENSE)_____

NOUN _____

VERB (PAST TENSE)_____

NOUN _____

PLURAL NOUN _____

MAD LIBS

THE THREE LITTLE PIGS

Once upon a time, there were three little pigs who decided to build

themselves houses. The first pig was _____, and he built

ADJECTIVE

his house out of _____. The second pig worked very

PLURAL NOUN

_____ and built a house out of _____. But

ADVERB   PLURAL NOUN

the third pig was _____. He built his house out of

ADJECTIVE

_____ and _____. Then one day a big wolf came

PLURAL NOUN   TYPE OF LIQUID

along. When he saw the first pig's house, he _____ and he

VERB (PAST TENSE)

_____ until he blew it down. Then he blew down the sec-

VERB (PAST TENSE)

ond pig's _____. But no matter how hard he _____,

NOUN   VERB (PAST TENSE)

he couldn't blow down the third pig's _____.

NOUN

MORAL: Once the _____ come home to roost, it's too late

PLURAL NOUN

to whitewash the walls.

MAD LIBS® is fun to play with friends, but you can also play it by yourself! To begin with, DO NOT look at the story on the page below. Fill in the blanks on this page with the words called for. Then, using the words you have selected, fill in the blank spaces in the story.

Now you've created your own hilarious MAD LIBS® game!

THE POOR SPOTTED AUK

PLURAL NOUN _____

PLURAL NOUN _____

ADJECTIVE _____

ADJECTIVE _____

ANIMAL _____

PLURAL NOUN _____

PLURAL NOUN _____

NOUN _____

ADJECTIVE _____

ADJECTIVE _____

MAD LIBS
THE POOR SPOTTED AUK

The auk is a bird which will soon be extinct because hunters keep

shooting it so they can sell its _____ to women who wear
                                   PLURAL NOUN

them on their _____. The government should establish
                 PLURAL NOUN

_____ game preserves where auks can build nests and lay
   ADJECTIVE

eggs and where they would be safe from their natural enemies, the

_____ otter and the underwater _____. Others
   ADJECTIVE   ANIMAL

sneak up and eat the poor auk's _____. Of course, a female
                                    PLURAL NOUN

auk can lay five thousand _____ a year, and if they all hatched,
                             PLURAL NOUN

in a short time we would all be up to our _____ in auks.
                                              NOUN

Remember, a/an _____ auk is a/an _____ auk.
                  ADJECTIVE   ADJECTIVE

MAD LIBS® is fun to play with friends, but you can also play it by yourself! To begin with, DO NOT look at the story on the page below. Fill in the blanks on this page with the words called for. Then, using the words you have selected, fill in the blank spaces in the story.

Now you've created your own hilarious MAD LIBS® game!

LINK TRAINERS AND FLYING

ADJECTIVE _____

NOUN _____

PLURAL NOUN _____

NOUN _____

PLURAL NOUN _____

NOUN _____

ADJECTIVE _____

NOUN _____

NOUN _____

NOUN _____

NOUN _____

COLOR _____

NUMBER _____

NUMBER _____

MAD LIBS®
LINK TRAINERS AND FLYING

A Link Trainer is a/an _____ airplane that never leaves the
                         ADJECTIVE

_____ . It's used to teach beginning _____ the
      NOUN   PLURAL NOUN

principles of flying. It has a/an _____ and a full set of
                                        NOUN

_____ , just like a regular airplane. It can imitate any
   PLURAL NOUN

sort of aerial maneuver such as a loop-the- _____ or a/an
                                                    NOUN

_____ dive, and it is very safe. Nothing can happen to you
   ADJECTIVE

unless, of course, you forget to fasten your safety _____ .
                                                          NOUN

Then you might fall out on your _____ .
                                      NOUN

After a student passes the tests on the Link Trainer, he then gets into

a real plane and learns to taxi down the _____ . And he
                                                NOUN

learns to tell which way the _____ is blowing before he
                                   NOUN

takes off into the "Wild _____ Yonder!" Then, in no time,
                              COLOR

he learns to take off and is flying _____ miles per hour at a
                                         NUMBER

height of _____ feet. When he does this, he is a real pilot.
              NUMBER

MAD LIBS® is fun to play with friends, but you can also play it by yourself! To begin with, DO NOT look at the story on the page below. Fill in the blanks on this page with the words called for. Then, using the words you have selected, fill in the blank spaces in the story.

Now you've created your own hilarious MAD LIBS® game!

FIRE FIGHTERS

ADJECTIVE_____

ADJECTIVE_____

NOUN _____

NOUN _____

PLURAL NOUN _____

NUMBER _____

PLURAL NOUN _____

NOUN _____

NOUN _____

ADJECTIVE_____

TYPE OF LIQUID _____

PLURAL NOUN _____

ADJECTIVE_____

NOUN _____

MAD LIBS®
FIRE FIGHTERS

When I was ten years old, my _____ ambition in life was
                                    ADJECTIVE

to be a fire fighter — but here I am, nothing but a/an _____
                                                         ADJECTIVE

_____ . If I were a fire fighter, I'd get to wear a huge, red
   NOUN

_____ . And I could ride on the fire engines that carry 80-foot
   NOUN

_____ and travel _____ miles an hour. When fire engines
 PLURAL NOUN   NUMBER

blow their _____ , all cars have to pull over to the side of
            PLURAL NOUN

the _____ . Fire departments have hook and _____
      NOUN   NOUN

wagons as well as pump trucks which carry _____ hoses
                                              ADJECTIVE

that pump _____ into burning _____ . Fire
           TYPE OF LIQUID   PLURAL NOUN

fighters have to go into _____ buildings and fight their way
                          ADJECTIVE

through smoke and _____ to rescue any _____
                     NOUN   PLURAL NOUN

who may be trapped inside. We should all be thankful that our fire

fighters are on the job twenty-four hours a/an _____ .
                                                  NOUN

MAD LIBS® is fun to play with friends, but you can also play it by yourself! To begin with, DO NOT look at the story on the page below. Fill in the blanks on this page with the words called for. Then, using the words you have selected, fill in the blank spaces in the story.

Now you've created your own hilarious MAD LIBS® game!

SMOKING CIGARETTES

TYPE OF DISEASE _____

NOUN _____

PART OF THE BODY _____

ADJECTIVE _____

PERSON IN ROOM _____

PLURAL NOUN _____

PLURAL NOUN _____

NASTY ADJECTIVE _____

PLURAL NOUN _____

EXCLAMATION _____

PLURAL NOUN _____

MAD LIBS®
SMOKING CIGARETTES

Medical science has discovered that smoking cigarettes causes

_____ . It is also bad for your _____ and causes
TYPE OF DISEASE   NOUN

pains in the _____ . When mice and dogs were exposed
PART OF THE BODY

to _____ cigarette smoke, they developed _____'s
ADJECTIVE   PERSON IN ROOM

disease. Tobacco companies have put charcoal _____ on
PLURAL NOUN

the ends of cigarettes, but they still spend millions of _____ .
PLURAL NOUN

advertising their _____ product. If you smoke cigarettes,
NASTY ADJECTIVE

the tobacco will leave all kinds of tar and _____ in your
PLURAL NOUN

lungs. This will make you cough and say, "_____!"
EXCLAMATION

Don't smoke cigarettes. Remember, only _____ smoke.
PLURAL NOUN